Dear Sarah
I thank God for you!
Your book Dont Settle for Safe
helped me push pass my
fears of finishing my book.
I am grateful for every
transparent moment that
you've shared because it has
helped me become a better
servant and woman. Please
Continue to push and share
because we need you!
Your Big Sis
Kathy Taylor 2018

Praises for The Diary of a Grown-Up

The Diary of a Grown-Up portrays the mind, heart, and faith of the author and proves journal writing to be a helpful therapy and a personal fortress. A place where inner thoughts and feelings can be expressed safely in joy and sadness in a confused or confident state without outside influences and disturbance. This is by far one of the most transparent gender-neutral writings I've encountered. The reader can take a journey through the pages and discover "real life" talk resolved by the assurance of inspirational scriptures that reaffirm who and whose you are.

Sharonja Houston, Artist/Singer

People who are interested in recognizing themselves and how self impacts thinking is a key reason a person should pick up this book. This book speaks to everyone about their passage in life. It talks about a very familiar topic of brokenness and getting rid of our painful situations.

Readers can gain knowledge of what it was like to be in a state of loneliness and knowing that God is there with you. The book provides the specific scriptures, one can read and align themselves with when they are in certain situations in their lives. It highlights how a person should use faith along their journey and knowing your purpose in the darkest moments.

Dr. Maloney Hunter, Educator/Author

Praises for The Diary of a Grown-Up

The Diary of a Grown-Up addresses so many relevant topics for every and anyone who can honestly admit to the hurdles, setbacks and even the joy that life affords us. This book takes the reader on a journey. A journey of personal and spiritual reflection. This book is a refreshing opportunity for us to examine our past and see our current and future situation through a renewed lens.

I enjoyed every Chapter but personally connected with Chapter 6, "She is Something Extra." As women we often struggle with fully letting our light shine and owning our greatness. We're often afraid we'll appear cocky or arrogant. But, this poem reminds us that it's ok to own and acknowledge your value and that you are Something Extra!

This book is a great read and can be a great gift for folks at every stage of adulthood!

Aleea S. Slappy, Business Development Manager-
City Of Norfolk

The Diary of a Grown-Up

The Diary of a Grown-Up

Embracing the Changes and Challenges That Come with Growth and Life

Kathy Taylor

Printed in the United States of America
First Printing, 2018
ISBN 13: 978-1-7321665-0-9

For bulk orders contact us at TheDiaryOfAGrownup@gmail.com
www.TheDiaryOfAGrownup.com
www.IAmSomethingExtra.com

Credits:
Book Cover designed: If You Brand It
Author Photo: Lori Vann
Edited: Ebi Johnson

Dedication

This book is dedicated to every adult that has made the choice not to give up on life and God. To every woman who continues to move forward even when shifts and changes seem to put you two steps behind. To every man that steps up and accepts the challenge to be focused on his future instead of dwelling on his past.

To my mom and dad who support and love me. To my business mentor for pushing me to finish this book. To my pastor, Dr. Kirk T. Houston Sr., and my Gethsemane Community Fellowship Baptist Church family. Thank you for modeling compassion, kindness, and love for all people.

CONTENTS

Foreword

It gives me great pleasure to have been afforded the opportunity to read The Diary of a Grown-Up. It is quite apparent that a tremendous amount of work and thought went into its' production. Bringing this book to fruition, required years of experiences and life encounters. Thought provoking questions are raised regarding what it means to become an adult. Kathy's words seemly emphasize that adulthood is not solely based upon an individual's age but rather upon the maturity level of the individual. She encourages the reader not to merely look towards a "village" for guidance but rather to look to the chief of all "villages". The Lord God, our Maker and Creator, He and He alone has the blueprints and the master plan for our lives.

We are all unique persons, fearfully and wonderfully crafted by the Master's hand; however, we still share similar scenarios in life. The Diary of a Grown-Up addresses a multiplicity of adult topics and propels the reader to move out of his or her feelings, and to step out on faith. The reader comes to the realization that there is always room for improvement and that a good self-evaluation includes room for refinement. Road blocks named Vulnerability and Denial may obstruct our paths from time to time, but we must remember our Purpose and not become sidetracked by our emotions.

I personally found the book to be light and witty while at the same wise and weighty. Tough topics were addressed by placing a little sugar on the tip of the spoon making the topic easier to swallow. Catchy titles drew the reader into the writing and caused the reader to assume ownership and confess to the truths that were contained within. If the reader had only three words to describe this rich work, those words would be enriching, enthralling, and empowering.

The Diary of a Grown-Up would prove to be excellent supplemental material for a young adult bible study or discussion. The book is laden with tad bits of wisdom and quotations from God's Word. Kathy has taken the liberty of putting flesh and blood upon adult situations and causes the reader to view being a grown-up through the "eyes" of God and contemplate maturity through the "mind" of God. Adulthood is full of processes. Processes are full of stages. Complete the process by completing the stage. May we continue to grow on this journey and not miss the beauty of it, while trying to get to the destination.

Congratulations to my daughter for the completion of this work. You have done well. It has been a pleasure observing you blossom into the beautiful woman that you are. I taught you the best I could but some things you had to learn on your own. This book is evidence that you are on the right path. Love and much success in all your future endeavors.

Rev. Janice D. Spellman, BA, MA
aka
Mom

Introduction

Dear Reader,

There is just no way to communicate or explain the responsibilities that being a grown up brings. Life as an adult has exceeded everything that I could imagine! I am not just talking about difficulties and hardships. I mean the joys of life that come with completing certain goals, as well. Even as I get older, I am still unsure of my next move. More episodes of "life happens" are released, and I find myself binge-watching my life as it unfolds. I start recapping the past, scanning the present, and anticipating my future episodes. The dangers of watching my life is just that - I am watching, instead of being an active participant in a leading role. I have often felt like I was living as an outsider, yelling at the woman making so many mistakes. It's as if I am in the audience watching a drama or horror flick screaming, "Don't go in there!" or "Why can't you see he's not the one?" Many times, I have thought, I wish I could save her! Then, the reality of it all kicks in, and I remember that I am her, and I can save her. Well, at least I am connected to someone who can. See, there is a beautiful part of this story that helps bring hope to all the uncertainties. That hope is my relationship with God. The more I depend on Him and turn away from doing things my way, the more I am able to enjoy the journey.

-Kathy

The Diary of a Grown-Up is a compilation of poems, essays, and expressions relating to a variety of events that happen to grown-ups. It is about embracing the changes and challenges that come with growth and life. Each chapter is related to experiences and decisions that the average adult must make. The goal is to inspire, empower, and remind adults to have faith, and to trust God throughout their journey in life.

In the beginning of each chapter I took a moment to share my personal thoughts about the topic. It is my hope that every reader will find a chapter or two that resonates with them and then make the choice to dig deeper into expressing their own views, feelings, and emotions. Use the Dear Diary section after each chapter to jot down your thoughts and ideas. Start a conversation and connect the dots in your own life about your feelings. When your thoughts turn into words, your actions are set in motion which will determine your future success. I wish you well as you push forward towards pursuing your purpose with God.

1

Vulnerability...

Be Aware of the Cover-Up

Dear Diary,

Being vulnerable takes a lot of courage. It connects us to others and God. Unfortunately, I often block that connection with a self-protective shield, creating a barrier between me and others. That barrier keeps me from experiencing healthy relationships, and the intimacy that I both need and desire. When I am open and vulnerable with others I can face my fears and begin asking for what I need. I now recognize that this is the glue that holds relationships together. If vulnerability is the willingness to show up and be seen, I know that I cannot be authentically known if I'm paralyzed by the fear of what people might see, say, or do. If I start naming the cause of my shame or fear, and speak about them, they will begin to disappear.

-Kathy

Shame only works when you believe that you are alone in your situation. When you choose to be vulnerable enough to expose yourself to others, you will experience a greater understanding than you could have ever imagined. Choosing to be resilient can help you share things and learn that we all have something in common. Everyone at some point is going to experience being embarrassed, personally attacked, offended, or shamed. We must make the choice to become more resilient and live free of the what-ifs of life.

2 Corinthians 12:9 (NIV) "But he said to me, "My grace is sufficient for you, for my power is made perfect in weakness." Therefore, I will boast all the more gladly about my weaknesses, so that Christ's power may rest on me."

Galatians 6:1-10 (MSG) "Live creatively, friends. If someone falls into sin, forgivingly restore him, saving your critical comments for yourself. You might be needing forgiveness before the day's out. Stoop down and reach out to those who are oppressed. Share their burdens, and so complete Christ's law. If you think you are too good for that, you are badly deceived."

The Cover Story

The new purse matches perfectly to those stilettos that prop her legs at a perfect angle.
I won't even mention the diamond earrings and the Swarovski bangle.
The class and style of this woman are known and admired by many.
The secret life that she lives wouldn't be believed by any.
Nobody knows the trouble she sees.
Nobody knows her sorrow.
Nobody will ever know the real trouble she feels.
Most don't care as long as she appears to be fly tomorrow.
The cover of her book is designed with attention to fine details.
The inside of her book makes her feel like she's living in hell!
He is the epitome of tall, dark, and handsome.
Women fumble over words just from his "hello".
He is envied and hated by many, yet still remains calm and mellow.
The way he walks and his smile, makes you want to hang out with him a while.
Every woman thinks they are going to be 'the one'.
They have no idea of the inner torment he faces after the sun.
Nobody knows the trouble he sees.
Nobody knows his sorrow.
Nobody will ever know the real trouble he feels.
As long as they catch a glimpse of him tomorrow.
His cover is sleek with the right color blend.

The inside of his book won't let him feel he can freely repent from his sins!

The facade of the covers provided a smoke and mirrors effect. The inside of those covers is where the true measurements of a person's heart can be found! You cannot follow the ways of others if you want to truly be the individual that God created you to be.

James 5:16 (GNT) "So then, confess your sins to one another and pray for one another, so that you will be healed. The prayer of a good person has a powerful effect."

Jude 20-25 (GNT) "and keep yourselves in the love of God, as you wait for our Lord Jesus Christ in his mercy to give you eternal life. Show mercy toward those who have doubts; save others by snatching them out of the fire; and to others show mercy mixed with fear, but hate their very clothes, stained by their sinful lusts."

These Eyes

He asked, "What are you thinking about?"
I asked, "Why'd you ask?"
He said, "When I looked at your eyes, they seemed clear as glass."
I didn't know how to respond, so I pretended to laugh and joke.
He looked at me seriously and said, "Now they are filled with smoke!"
I got annoyed and said, "What do you mean by that?"
He said, "You can't hide the truth by throwing out useless facts."
Those words rung deep in my ears and the river of tears started to flow.
I begin thinking. But how...and what does He really know?
I didn't speak a word out loud, yet He responded to my every thought.
He said, "I know everything about you. My life was traded, and your sins were bought."
The rush of peace that overtook my mind was beyond anything I could explain.
These eyes have seen so much; however, His love heals all my pain!

Romans 8:26-28 (MSG) "Meanwhile, the moment we get tired in the waiting, God's Spirit is right alongside helping us along. If we don't know how or what to pray, it doesn't matter. He does our praying in and for us, making prayer out of our wordless sighs, our aching groans. He knows us far better than we know ourselves, knows our pregnant condition, and keeps us present before God. That's why we can be so sure that every detail in our lives of love for God is worked into something good."

Alternative Facts or Faith

Sometimes, the facts that you are faced with contradict what you believe. Do you believe what you hear in the natural, or will you believe what God said? The word alternative means having a choice of available possibilities. Quite the opposite, facts are information used as the only source of evidence. They are the truth. Here are five points that keep me focused on my faith that prevent alternative facts from distracting me.

1. **Be anxious for nothing.** We live in a society that tells us to act fast or be prepared to miss out on the next big thing. Do not confuse this with procrastination or feel the need to react quickly under pressure.

- Philippians 4:6-7: Do not be anxious about anything, but in every situation, by prayer and petition, with thanksgiving, present your requests to God. And the peace of God, which transcends all understanding, will guard your hearts and your minds in Christ Jesus.
- Matthew 6:33-34: But seek first his kingdom and his righteousness, and all these things will be given to you as well. Therefore, do not worry about tomorrow, for tomorrow will worry about itself. Each day has enough trouble of its own.
- Romans 8:28: And we know that in all things God works for the good of those who love him, who have been called according to his purpose.

2. **Be prayerful about everything.** We often say we prayed about "it". However, that could be an alternative fact. In actuality, you told God what, how, when, and why you wanted "it", and then you moved on without waiting for an answer.

- 1 Thessalonians 5:16-18: Rejoice always, pray continually, give thanks in all circumstances; for this is God's will for you in Christ Jesus.
- Proverbs 3:5-6: Trust in the Lord with all your heart and lean not on your own understanding; in all your ways submit to him, and he will make your paths straight.

3. **Be open and flexible.** We know what we like, and if it isn't broke why should we try to fix it, or allow anyone else to disrupt the flow, and change it? This kind of thinking only keeps us stuck and limited in our growth. We must give God room to move in and through us.

- Luke 9:23: Then he said to them all: "Whoever wants to be my disciple must deny themselves and take up their cross daily and follow me."
- Philippians 3:12-14: Not that I have already obtained all this, or have already arrived at my goal, but I press on to take hold of that for which Christ Jesus took hold of me. Brothers and sisters, I do not consider myself yet to have taken hold of it. But one thing I do: Forgetting what is behind and straining toward what is ahead, I press on toward the goal to win the prize for which God has called me heavenward in Christ Jesus.

4. **Be happy.** Do you want to be right, or do you want to be happy? Everything does not always require a response or comment. Sometimes, it is better to release it and move forward.

- Galatians 5:22-25: But the fruit of the Spirit is love, joy, peace, forbearance, kindness, goodness, faithfulness, gentleness, and self-control. Against such things, there is no law. Those who belong to Christ Jesus have crucified the flesh with its passions and desires. Since we live by the Spirit, let us keep in step with the Spirit.

5. **Be grateful**. We should be grateful that we don't have to do life or figure things out alone. In those moments when my facts are clouding my thoughts and faith, I must remember Jeremiah 29:11.

- Jeremiah 29:11: "For I know the plans I have for you," declares the Lord, "plans to prosper you and not to harm you, plans to give you hope and a future."

Join me in believing what God says about you. Let your faith and confidence in God overpower the available possibilities, as well as information received by others.

Hebrews 11 (NIV) "Now faith is confidence in what we hope for and assurance about what we do not see."

The Conversation

It's a back and forth dialogue.
It requires giving and taking.
It takes talking as well as listening.
It will require digesting some information that was not anticipated.
It can cause a series of emotions to manifest.
It may take restraint and discipline.
It can lead to the next time.
It can lead to a never again!

James 1:19 (AMP) "Understand this, my beloved brothers and sisters. Let everyone be quick to hear [be a careful, thoughtful listener], slow to speak [a speaker of carefully chosen words and], slow to anger [patient, reflective, forgiving]."

Where are you God?

For He was wounded for me.

He took stripes and whips for me.

Because of His suffering, I am healed.

I am delivered!

I am free!

In the middle of my pain, He was there.

In the middle of my uncertainties, He was there.

In the middle of my heartache, He was there.

Right now, He is here.

Right now, He is healing me.

Right now, He is healing me from unseen dangers.

Right now, He is in love with me.

He will bless my future days.

He will show me favor.

He will extend grace.

He will deliver me from harm.

I am covered by Him!

Isaiah 53:5 (KJV) "But he was wounded for our transgressions, he was bruised for our iniquities: the chastisement of our peace was upon him; and with his stripes we are healed."

The Lover of My Soul

This kind of love runs deep within.
It cannot be duplicated by other men.
There is a special connection between us.
In order to understand it, you have to trust.
Trust in what you think is real.
Trust what you cannot see but can feel.
This level of vulnerability exposes you to the core.
This kind of love says shame can dwell within you no more!
This love is patient and kind.
This love says He's a true friend of mine.
My soul rejoices at the mere thought of You.
I am grateful for your love and I love you too!

1 John 4:16-18 (NIV) "And so we know and rely on the love God has for us. God is love. Whoever lives in love lives in God, and God in them. This is how love is made complete among us so that we will have confidence on the day of judgment: In this world we are like Jesus. There is no fear in love. But perfect love drives out fear, because fear has to do with punishment. The one who fears is not made perfect in love."

Hide and Seek

She told herself that she did not need help, because she could do it all alone.
One day she realized she needed help, but everyone was gone.
She covered her disappointment and pain with a Strong Independent Woman shirt.
That shirt was not long enough because depressed, and lonely were written all over her skirt.
She put a lot of time in trying to hide the way she feels.
Nobody was supposed to know that when alone at night, it is hard for her to even deal!
She cannot even communicate the extent she goes to hide her shame.
It is impossible to share the past because you would not be able to call her by name!
How in the world could she seek help after all that she has done?
Who would volunteer to help her other than God the Father, and Son?
She started with a prayer out of desperation and fear.
She received the peace that surpassed her understanding, and now her thoughts are clear.
She is no longer in hiding, because she chose to seek God's way.
Her story inspires others, and she is grateful for His love every day.

Psalms 34:4 (NIV) "I sought the LORD, and he answered me; he delivered me from all my fears."

Dear Diary,

Reading through this chapter has made me recognize ...

2

Healing From Your DNA

Denial aNd Adversity

Dear Diary,

I know that God is not complicated. Even though things may not always make sense in my mind, I must remind myself that God is not the author of confusion. When He created me, His plan was not to make my life difficult or full of drama and obstacles. He created me and designed me with a specific plan for my life. My job is to believe in the plan and trust the process.

-Kathy

It does not matter how high your self-esteem is or how much you value yourself. When you experience rejection, it stings. I know many motivational speakers, and empowerment coaches will tell you to "pull yourself up by your bootstraps" or that "this too shall pass". They are right to a certain level because you do have to figure out how to move forward. A great place to start is with the truth. There is some form of truth attached to most stories. Learning how to include the truth will give you freedom from F.E.A.R. (False Evidence Appearing Real). The truth will allow you to become a better version of yourself, and it will help you navigate through the hurt and pain attached. If you say "yes" to God's plan, purpose, and way even when you don't understand the "whys", He'll provide grace, mercy, and favor beyond your understanding. Regardless of your past mistakes and detours in life, He is always willing to give you a fresh start, if you ask.

Psalm 34:19 (NIV) "The righteous person may have many troubles, but the Lord delivers him from them all."

James 1:2-4 (NIV) "Consider it pure joy, my brothers and sisters, whenever you face trials of many kinds, because you know that the testing of your faith produces perseverance. Let perseverance finish its work so that you may be mature and complete, not lacking anything.

Goodbye Pain

I have ignored you and pretended that you did not exist for way too long.

You showed up uninvited and stayed past your welcome.

I ducked and dodged you instead of facing the core of your being.

You brought company and invited them to stay because I became afraid to call you out.

Layers upon layers of hurt, fear, and shame have been built on your foundation.

Your charismatic ways made me feel that there is no need to change since you no longer bother me daily.

You convinced me to focus on current situations and let the past stay in the past.

As I learn and grow, I understand that unless I deal with the past, it will continue to take root in my future.

I am not in denial anymore, and I am serving "pain" its eviction notice.

Today, I am free from every excuse, chain, and form of bondage that has kept me bound!

We can press on each day knowing that our God loves us and wants to use the hurt and pain in this world to bring Him glory.

Psalm 34:18 (MSG) "If your heart is broken, you'll find God right there; if you're kicked in the gut, he'll help you catch your breath."

Revelation 21:4 (NIV) "He will wipe every tear from their eyes. There will be no more death or mourning or crying or pain, for the old order of things has passed away."

Let It Go

I am going to be fine.

I am too blessed to be stressed.

I don't do drama.

Most people have used some phrase that embodies the fact that they know how to "let it go" when needed. The truth is, we all have a way of covering up things that we don't want to address. Continually ignoring things and dismissing how we truly feel is a recipe for self-destruction. Let's explore what it means to really "let it go."

LET

Truth does not triumph by convincing someone to believe your perspective. Similarly, telling yourself something over and over again does not negate the truth about a situation or circumstance. We must Learn not to Exclude the Truth (L.E.T.). One must gain the knowledge and appropriate skills in order to learn something. If someone or something is not taken into account, they have been excluded. In this case, that someone is you and that something is your truth.

1 Corinthians 13:11 (NIV) "When I was a child, I talked like a child, I thought like a child, I reasoned like a child. When I became a man, I put the ways of childhood behind me."

The things you did as a teenager can no longer fly. Relationships, friendships, and business transactions cannot be handled the way they have been handled in the past. When you know better, you should do better. Or be prepared to suffer the consequences of doing childlike things with grown-ups. Telling fibs, white lies, or fairy tales seem like a harmless solution at times. But keep in mind that when you lie to others, you also lie to yourself. And there is no way of being free from fear if you lie to yourself! The superficial you will eventually self-destruct on this path. You deserve the best version of you, so be true to you. Even if you fear it will hurt someone else's feelings. People are resilient, and they will readjust if, and when, they are honest with themselves. Essentially, when you exclude the truth, you slam the door in the face of your authentic happiness. Use this opportunity to evaluate certain areas of your life that need immediate help and start there.

Affirmation: I will celebrate me by accepting my truth!

IT

Everyone has or will experience some form of trauma in their lifetime. Internal Trauma (I.T.) is the emotional damage that results from extremely stressful or disturbing experiences. Thankfully, with God's help we can recover from it! However, we can continue to suffer from things left unaddressed, plaguing us from within.

There are two main types of trauma: blunt trauma and penetrating trauma. An example of blunt trauma is an injury that incurred in a car accident, or from a baseball flying at high speed. The skin is likely unbroken, but there is internal bruising and other damage. The blood vessels inside the body are usually torn or crushed by sheer force, or from a blunt object. An example of penetrating trauma is trauma from a bullet injury. Here are two examples of the role trauma plays in common life experiences:

- You are in a monogamous relationship with the love of your life, until you find out that he/she has another family or relationship. You are devastated because you have been emotionally and physically invested in this person for quite some time. Despite all of this, you really don't want to let them go. So, you begin to rationalize their excuses and deny the truth. You know who God says you are but it's easier to hold onto a superficial situation. You move forward, or so you think, by saying, "Oh, I'm okay" and ignore the pain that's buried deep within. Until you finally scream from the blunt force hit of that devastating news. While the hit may have been unexpected, the denial, suppression and lack of care caused the real damage.

- You and your supervisor are friends and you are frequently 5-10 minutes late. She never says anything because she too is usually running a few minutes late. As you settle at your desk and check your Inbox, you notice an email that wasn't meant for you. However, you and the position you recently applied for are the topic of discussion. Your supervisor states that she will not recommend you for the position due to numerous concerns. The same supervisor who seemed like such a blessing now sounds like a curse! You are so floored by the knife that was stuck in your back that you can't even catch your breath! You look up at the cute little WWJD sign hanging on the wall and decide to dismiss it and keep your distance. Fast forward several weeks later. Your supervisor walks by and says, "Oh, you look nice today," and you black out and proceed to curse her out! Everyone is shocked, and you are immediately terminated. Since you ignored the pain and did not seek help for that "penetrating wound" of betrayal, it got infected. The effects of internal trauma pushed you into a new level of pain. Now, you are jobless and emotionally broken.

These scenarios may not be relatable; however, as a grown-up, there will be a life experience that leaves you internally traumatized at some point. Life is full of challenges that bring us closer to God. And whether we realize it or not, we all have scars, because we've all been through something. I encourage you to call on God first, so He can provide the aide that you need. If we looked like what we have been through, some of us wouldn't be recognizable.

Psalms 46:1 "God is our refuge and strength, an ever-present help in trouble."

Affirmation: I will acknowledge and accept the facts to heal from the inside out!

GO

Did you ever reveal to someone your dream business plan, and shortly after telling them, you realize that they aren't as excited about it as you had hoped? Or have you ever shared your amazing idea with someone who made you feel like it was an impossible task? Sure, you could press past the naysayers. Except, you haven't seen any real progress in making your dream happen. And even though it has been a frustrating and discouraging process, you still can't shake the idea.

This is common for exceptionally creative people who think beyond current times, or who are unable to sort out all of their ideas. I call this Genius Overload (G.O.).

There is no true or precise definition for the word genius. It all comes down to one's own emphasis on their creativity and/or eminent achievements. When you identify your gift, and purpose and choose to get laser-focused on just that, something amazing will take root and grow. There is a specific purpose inside of you. Many of the problems that cripple our world remain unresolved because people are not fulfilling their purpose. Watch the daily news. Read the paper. Talk to someone! The world needs you to fulfill that purpose with aggressive intentions. God gave the solution to someone. Is that person you? Do you have an idea that could potentially help our children, our communities, our country?

Genesis 1:1 "In the beginning, God created the Heaven and Earth."

God already knew what you were supposed to do from the very beginning when He created the heavens and the earth. It wasn't by chance that you were created. It's not by happenstance or luck that you have this idea that you can't seem to shake. Regardless of how many times you pick it up and put it down, the mere thought of doing it still gives you life! You were made to do this.

When you LET IT GO and LEARN not to EXCLUDE the TRUTH, you can heal from the INTERNAL TRAUMA, and the GENIUS in you will not get OVERLOADED because you will produce the greatness inside of you!

A Father's Love

How can I be there for him when he wasn't there for me?
I thought I had gotten over this until I heard him cry for the first time.
There is a responsibility that comes with him being all mine!
An overwhelming feeling came over me thinking, I'm not ready for this.
That was all washed away with the feeling of his head on my chest.
WOW!
Fatherhood is such a beautiful blessing, so how could he turn it into a curse.
I have tried to get answers, but I just keep reliving the hurt.
I hope, wish, and pray that I do not get the urge to run off in fear.
After all he did it, and I made it through the silent tears.
He was not there for me, so how can I be there for him?
God's love, and mercy gives me beyond what my biological father could give.
I am breaking the cycle, and in the past I shall no longer live!
I will be there by showing up one day at a time.
I can be there by never letting him forget that he is mine.
In the good times and bad, I will be there for my son.
I will let God's love serve as my role model on how it's done.

Psalm 68:5-6 (NIV) "A father to the fatherless, a defender of widows, is God in his holy dwelling. God sets the lonely in families, he leads out the prisoners with singing; but the rebellious live in a sun-scorched land.

Broken BUT Better

Sometimes if we spend time thinking about the things we have done, places we have been, and things we have said, we can find ourselves stricken with regret. We start dwelling on the "whys" of life:
Why didn't I go to college?
Why did I stay in that unhealthy relationship?
Why did I let the voice of others dictate who I should be?

When we allow ourselves to stay in this questionable state, we become broken, and that actually presents a perfect opportunity for God to help us. It is hard to imagine how we can bounce back from some of the obstacles we've faced. Especially, when it feels like we were part of the problem. But your Creator is the only one who knows exactly who you are and who you are supposed to be. When you feel broken about any area of your life, even if you think the situation is beyond repair, pull out the owner's manual and call technical support. The Bible is your owner's manual, and prayer is your technical support. People can give suggestions, and maybe even assist you along the way, but no one can fix or restore you like the one who made you. Know that even when you feel broken, you are going through the healing process of getting better.
Mark 11:24-25 (GNT) "For this reason I tell you: When you pray and ask for something, believe that you have received it, and you will be given whatever you ask for. And when you stand and pray, forgive anything you may have against anyone, so that your Father in heaven will forgive the wrongs you have done."

That Day That You Needed an Answer

Even though you are screaming out loud, it seems like you are only whispering through the tears that flood your face, the pounding hurt in your chest, and the anguish and insane thoughts in your head. You don't want to retell or relive any aspect of this feeling again.

You keep asking yourself:

What can I say to get relief?

When will the pain end?

Where shall I go to get help?

How do I release this hurt?

Why do I even exist?

All these questions, and no answers. Everyone just says, "It will be okay." But even when you can't see a way out, take a moment to look up! God is able to do just what He said He would. He will fulfill every promise He made. He said, "I will never leave nor forsake you." So, in the moments when you can't figure out the "what", "when", "where", and "how", trust the One who said He will be with you always.

Psalm 103:1-5 (NKJV) "Bless the Lord, O my soul; And all that is within me, bless His holy name! Bless the Lord, O my soul, and forget not all His benefits: forgives all your iniquities, Who heals all your diseases, Who redeems your life from destruction, Who crowns you with lovingkindness and tender mercies, Who satisfies your mouth with good things, So that your youth is renewed like the eagle's."

Let Your Faith Overpower Your Feelings

It is okay to tell God exactly how you feel. Pour out your heart to Him. Unload every emotion that you are feeling. God can handle your doubt, anger, fear, grief, confusion, and every question you may have.

You may be thinking; "how do I praise God when I do not understand what is happening in my life and God seems silent? How do I stay connected in a crisis? How do I keep my eyes on Jesus when they are full of tears"?

Remember, He knows what you are thinking before you even say it. He is waiting for you to come to Him about that problem, concern, or secret desire that you hold so tightly. Give God the opportunity to show you the results of real faith and sincere prayers. It may not end the way you predicted, but it will be much better than anything you could have imagined. Loosen your grip and begin to release these feelings. Let God give you peace and fulfill His promises to you.

Joshua 1:9 (NIV) "Have I not commanded you? Be strong and courageous. Do not be afraid; do not be discouraged, for the Lord your God will be with you wherever you go."
2 Timothy 1:7 (NIV) "For the Spirit God gave us does not make us timid, but gives us power, love and self-discipline."

Let Not Your Heart Stay Troubled

Daily life obstacles tend to bring a variety of hardships and pain.
It can get rough and make you feel like you are going insane.
Do not allow yourself to get absorbed with the things that are not going right.
When you feel overwhelmed choose to push past that feeling and continue to fight!
The scripture says, "Joy cometh in the morning", and that is true.
You must remember that God's timing is not like the 24 hours for me and you.
Let not your heart stay troubled and remain in a panic state.
Remember God will always provide, and His way is worth the wait!

Psalm 30:1-5 (NIV) "I will exalt you, Lord, for you lifted me out of the depths and did not let my enemies gloat over me. Lord my God, I called to you for help, and you healed me. You, Lord, brought me up from the realm of the dead; you spared me from going down to the pit. Sing the praises of the Lord, you his faithful people; praise his holy name. For his anger lasts only a moment, but his favor lasts a lifetime; weeping may stay for the night, but rejoicing comes in the morning."

Thoughts of A Man

I am a man, so I do not cry.
I am a man, if they said I showed weakness, I'd call them a lie!
I am a man, I am strong as an ox.
I am a man, so I can get away with calling her a fox.
I am a man, I will never admit when I feel alone.
I am a man, so when you respond to me...watch your tone!
As a man, I disguise my feelings because of what I was taught.
When I was a boy, a different way is what I would have sought.
I am a man, and I have put away those childish ways.
They are the old me and now I see clearer days.
I am now a man that is focused on keeping it together.
I am now a man that will serve Christ forever!

1 Timothy 6:11 (NIV) "But you, man of God, flee from all this, and pursue righteousness, godliness, faith, love, endurance and gentleness."

Dear Diary,

Reading through this chapter has made me recognize ...

3

People Change, Not Your Purpose

Dear Diary,

I must remember that my purpose in life is specific and has been planned by God. When I allow people, places, and things to dictate my outcome or direction, I lose a piece of me. I must choose to look towards God instead of looking to those who choose to remind me of the times that I didn't value my purpose. Favor makes people who wanted to hate or curse me become key players in the blessing that has been waiting for me. God uses unthinkable ways and unusual circumstances to provide for me. I must stay in sync with His will regardless of my lack of understanding of the process.

-Kathy

It may take you some time to truly understand what loyalty means. In fact, you may have to redefine it in order to move forward. Many relationships start one way and end in a completely different way. People change. The very person that you may be trying to stay true to, could also be the very person responsible for causing conflict in your life. It is also possible for people with good intentions to cause you pain. Don't take all opposition as a sign or excuse to look at everyone suspiciously. Instead, allow the peace of God's word to be the determining factor of your sacred circle. Your relationship with God is most important. He can restore, repair, and renew you despite obstacles or crippling experiences. And you will reap His favor. You can't earn, buy, or save up for the experience that God will provide for you. Your purpose is pre-planned, and you are destined for greatness!

Romans 8:28 (GNT) "We know that in all things God works for good with those who love him, and those whom he has called according to his purpose."

Ephesians 4:32 (KJV) "And be ye kind one to another, tenderhearted, forgiving one another, even as God for Christ's sake hath forgiven you."

There Is a Blessing in the Lesson

This particular obstacle hurts so bad!
This pain makes you feel an abundance of hurt that is way beyond just sad.
You continue to think how, or why it happened this way.
You must search for reasons to get up and live yet another day.
Praying and encouraging words cannot even sink in right now.
You are just trying to remember how.
How to daily get out of bed.
How to keep those crazy thoughts out of your head!
Someone said you must have a test in order to have a testimony.
Your response is, "This kind of hurt feels horrific" so you can't front or be phony.
Days turned to night and the cycle starts again.
One day you felt like smiling, and that was the beginning of your "when".
When you sent praises up, blessing began to come down.
When you read God's word it brought hope, so you no longer needed to frown.
There's a blessing in the lesson if you want to learn.
There comes a time that you must fight for what you want to earn!
2 Corinthians 4:8-10 (NIV) "We are hard pressed on every side, but not crushed; perplexed, but not in despair; persecuted, but not abandoned; struck down, but not destroyed. 10 We always carry around in our body the death of Jesus, so that the life of Jesus may also be revealed in our body."

To Whom Much Is Given, Much Is Required

When you are living according to God's will and doing things to help His people, be prepared for all hell to break loose at times. To whom much is given, much is required. During the storm, don't run for cover and miss out on your overflow of blessings. Embrace the downpour and begin your best praise right there in the rain. Others may think you are crazy, but remain steadfast and ask God to send His angels to serve as your umbrella, so that you can continue to move forward safely in the storm.

2 Samuel 6:14(GNT) "David, wearing only a linen cloth around his waist, danced with all his might to honor the LORD."
Hebrews 10:35-39 (MSG) "Remember those early days after you first saw the light? Those were the hard times! Kicked around in public, targets of every kind of abuse—some days it was you, other days your friends. If some friends went to prison, you stuck by them. If some enemies broke in and seized your goods, you let them go with a smile, knowing they couldn't touch your real treasure. Nothing they did bothered you, nothing set you back. So, don't throw it all away now. You were sure of yourselves then. It's still a sure thing! But you need to stick it out, staying with God's plan so you'll be there for the promised completion. It won't be long now, he's on the way; he'll show up most any minute. But anyone who is right with me thrives on loyal trust; if he cuts and runs, I won't be very happy. But we're not quitters who lose out. Oh, no! We'll stay with it and survive, trusting all the way.

Who Are "They" Anyway?

They said this.
They said that.
Who are they?
Where are they at?
He said, and she said always spreading gossip around town.
Whenever they come to me with the nonsense, I immediately shut it down!
I've been there...and I've done that, too.
I've learned the lesson that what they're saying about me...they're also saying it about you!

Ephesians 4:28-32 (NLV) "If you are a thief, quit stealing. Instead, use your hands for good hard work, and then give generously to others in need. Don't use foul or abusive language. Let everything you say be good and helpful, so that your words will be an encouragement to those who hear them. And do not bring sorrow to God's Holy Spirit by the way you live. Remember, he has identified you as His own, guaranteeing that you will be saved on the day of redemption. Get rid of all bitterness, rage, anger, harsh words, and slander, as well as all types of evil behavior. Instead, be kind to each other, tenderhearted, forgiving one another, just as God through Christ has forgiven you."

Tolerance

I've been thinking back on the many ways that God has stretched me and prepared me for greatness. I have to confess — I don't always like some of the lessons that are incorporated into the process. One of those lessons is in the area of tolerance. Tolerance is an ability or willingness to accept someone, or something with an opinion, or behavior that is different from your own. The lessons on tolerance require a rewiring of the mind.

My Story

I was sitting in my vehicle writing at the beach when I looked up and saw birds gathering close by. An elderly couple parked next to me was feeding the birds french fries. They were amused by the birds' ability to swoop down and quickly grab the food. I, however, became instantly annoyed. Birds were flying from every direction and resting on my vehicle. As I was preparing to pull into a different parking spot, the word tolerance came to mind. You see, I really was not in harm's way. Nor was my vehicle being destroyed. I simply had a few seconds of inconvenience with one or two birds pecking at my vehicle and it became uncomfortable. I almost reacted harshly and irrationally about a simple situation. My thoughts shifted and so did my writing. I started to think and write about the many situations and concerns that are unsolved in this world. Imagine if we as a people could learn to live by this same lesson.

- What if instead of acting less out of frustration and fear of the unknown, we practiced being more tolerant of people's differences?

- What if instead of kicking people when they are down or when they make a mistake, we help them regain integrity and pride?
- What if we discipline and punish in private, while providing upliftment and prayer for all in public?
- What if we choose to live with love and peace even when no one is looking?

No one heard my thoughts or my grunt of frustration over the birds. No one would have cared about me moving to a different parking spot. The birds didn't care that I didn't feed them. They could easily fly to another area for food. I realized that just because I don't like a situation, or choose not to participate in it, doesn't mean that it's wrong. If I had not taken that moment to divert my thoughts, I would have missed this life lesson.

Romans 2:3-5 (GNT) "But you, my friend, do those very things for which you pass judgment on others! Do you think you will escape God's judgment? Or perhaps you despise his great kindness, tolerance, and patience. Surely you know that God is kind because he is trying to lead you to repent. But you have a hard and stubborn heart, and so you are making your own punishment even greater on the day when God's anger and righteous judgments will be revealed."

Don't Turn Your Blessing into a Curse

I was fed up with a business situation that I had been dealing with for a while. I love the power of words, so I decided to write a letter addressing my issue. I wanted the recipient of this letter to understand that I felt undervalued and as a result, the organization was about to lose a loyal team member. Basically, I was plotting to tell them off in a nice/nasty way.

I began to get my thoughts together and yet, I could not properly transfer them to paper. I envisioned this letter having a powerful yet eloquent sting to it. I even prayed for God to help me get a good flow of words together. And that's when I fell apart. I was reminded that I was asking God to bless my mess.

He gave me a good "talking to" and He reminded me of the increase I continuously prayed for. He reminded me of how I begged and pleaded with Him to let me meet people that share my life mission and goals. He played back a recording of my prayer for a career change and peace. God clearly asked me, "So what you're telling me is the things that are pushing you to accept the future changes have now caused those changes to seem like a curse?" God said that if He is providing the opportunities for me to move forward with His favor, why should I be so fixated on making someone else understand how they made me feel? Why give them credit for the change and not praising God for the blessing?

I am so grateful that even in my moments of ungrateful thinking, God continues to love me and show mercy. I choose to move forward and give God praise instead of putting emphasis on what someone else did. I am thankful for the uncomfortable situations because they help remind me that I can have peace even when I am pressed and comfortable. Those are the times that I will review His Words and His plans!

Dear Diary,

Reading through this chapter reminded me that my purpose is...

4

The "L" Word! Is it Love or Lust?

Dear Diary,

I know that love is patient, kind, forgiving, understanding, requires vulnerability, and so much more. Lust, on the other hand, is physical, intense, deceiving, anxious, and shameful. While love and lust have different descriptive adjectives, they often intertwine. Love and lust can produce a surface level attraction that leads to crossing the lines of unchartered territory. However, lust often dissolves when the "real person" is exposed. I have experienced both and as my relationship with God grows so does my descriptive for what loving myself and others look like. God has a way of making me feel protected and guarded when I sense trouble. He wipes away my tears when I feel sad. He attentively listens to me when I want to tell the long version of a story. Building a relationship with God has taught me how to be patient with myself. I am writing a new love story that has God in the leading role. Following His lead will keep me from making the same mistakes again.

-Kathy

Every day we must make choices, and even the simplest decisions can change the letters that come behind the "L". Let your love for God overpower your need to gratify your flesh in lust. God gives us a clear definition of love and lust.

1 Corinthians 13:4-7 (NIV) "Love is patient, love is kind. It does not envy, it does not boast, it is not proud. It does not dishonor others, it is not self-seeking, it is not easily angered, it keeps no record of wrongs. Love does not delight in evil but rejoices with the truth. It always protects, always trusts, always hopes, always perseveres."

Galatians 5:5-16 (NIV) "So I say, walk by the Spirit, and you will not gratify the desires of the flesh."

L-O-V-E

How can 4 letters carry so much weight?
The power of this word has the capability to transform the entire world.
LOVE can shift one's thoughts from negative to positive.
LOVE can create peace and harmony in the middle of hatred and strife.
LOVE sees the value in others.
LOVE promotes a cohesive energy.
LOVE thinks of others before self.
LOVE is not blind, it can see far beyond the current situation.
LOVE does not keep track of everything one did wrong.
LOVE is *L*iving *O*n *V*aluable *E*nergy!

Romans 12:9-10 (NIV) "Love must be sincere. Hate what is evil; cling to what is good. Be devoted to one another in love. Honor one another above yourselves."
Romans 13:10 (NIV) "Love does no harm to a neighbor. Therefore, love is the fulfillment of the law."

L-U-S-T

You never thought that you would be the one who yearned for someone and made decisions based on emotions.

The power and feeling of this word overcomes your thoughts, words, and actions at times.

LUST makes you long for someone in an unhealthy way.

LUST is an undeniable temptation that should not be taken lightly nor taken for granted.

LUST takes intimate connections and turns them into unforbidden fruit.

LUST will grab a hold of you and take over your flesh if you stay in denial.

LUST is Longing for an Undeniable Sensual Touch!

Psalm 101:3 (NIV) "I will not look with approval on anything that is vile. I hate what faithless people do; I will have no part in it."

1 John 2:16 (NIV) "For everything in the world the lust of the flesh, the lust of the eyes, and the pride of life comes not from the Father but from the world."

A Picture-Perfect Love

If I drew a picture of what love looked like, your face would appear.
The textures and colors capture the full beauty of your soul.
The shades and shadows showcase your heart intertwined with mine.
The defined outlines expose the essence of how protected I feel with you.
The framework would accent your strength.
The soft edges embody your character and values.
This picture is a masterpiece created with love.
This unduplicated art is indescribable to some and yet admired by many.
I had a vision of what love looked like, and you appeared.

You Tied My Soul in a Knot

You promised me!

You said it was a couple of forever's of just me and you.

You said someday we'd lock arms and before God and everyone say, "We do."

The connection was sealed with a lock and key to my heart.

The physical attraction could never part.

The mental ties that bonded us begin to unravel string by string.

My soul began to ache, and, in my ears, I heard a ring.

The sound of the beginning of the end of forever.

The ties, the promises, the connection of never.

My soul is tied in a tight knot that's hard to undo.

I just can't imagine how to do life without you!

A vulnerable state I now must face.

I called to God for His saving grace.

Lord, help my soul to release this hold.

You are the only one that can make this pain unfold.

Reminisce

As I look at your picture and think of you.

I think about what we used to do.

You know what I mean, play fighting and all.

Man, those were the days LOL...we had a ball!

I said "used to" because that was the past.

Now we have moved on, but sometimes...no lie, I wish it did last.

Well, let me shake off this backtracking because there is no happiness in that.

It ended for a reason and those are the real facts.

Two good people not good for each other.

My parting words are I wish you well ex-lover.

That Girl!

That girl who believes his lies,
That girl who helps him come up with an alibi.
That girl who tells him he's right, knowing he's dead wrong!
That girl who lives with the fairytale that y'all really do have a special song.
That girl who doesn't want to face reality because it hurts so bad.
That girl craving the man that she never really had.
That girl who thinks if she hopes and prays enough, her wish will come true.
Take a moment and think about if it did, he would probably just find another YOU!

Proverbs 31:30 (ESV) "Charm is deceitful, and beauty is vain, but a woman who fears the LORD is to be praised."

I Still Believe

I still believe in kind words and smiles.

I still believe in talking face to face for a while.

I still believe that love between man and woman exist.

I still believe in waiting before you kiss.

I still believe in chivalry and roles.

I still believe in holding doors and giving jackets when it is cold.

I still believe in taking our time.

I still believe in making your last name mine.

I still believe in having butterflies at the mention of your name.

I still believe that love does not create pain.

Some may not believe like I do.

I believe that he does, so is he you?

Dear Diary,

This chapter gave me some things to think about. I understand that love means....

5

LIFE with Others

Love Others

Invest in Others

Build a Future with Others

Encourage Others

Dear Diary,

Humility is not about thinking less of yourself. It's about thinking of yourself less. When you remove your ego from the situation and focus on leading and helping others you, in turn, will receive that same assistance. It's nice to be recognized; however, if your intention is solely to receive praise, you are totally missing the mark. You will continue to feel great disappointment when the attention you think you deserve isn't given. This brings into question who the attention should be on. Who are you doing this for? Society will make you think being humble or passive is related to your self-esteem and weakness. That is far from the truth and a trick that some try to keep embedded in their minds. Resist the devil and he will flee! One of the most powerful ways to bless others is by offering gentleness, meekness, and acts of humility when needed.

-Kathy

Matthew 6:1-4 (MSG) "Be especially careful when you are trying to be good so that you don't make a performance out of it. It might be good theater, but the God who made you won't be applauding. When you do something for someone else, don't call attention to yourself. You've seen them 'play-actors' I call them treating prayer meeting and street corner alike as a stage, acting compassionate as long as someone is watching, playing to the crowds. They get applause, but that's all they get. When you help someone out, do not think about how it looks. Just do it quietly and unobtrusively. That is the way your God, who conceived you in love, working behind the scenes, helps you out."

John 13:33-35 (MSG) "Let me give you a new command: Love one another. In the same way I loved you, you love one another. This is how everyone will recognize that you are my disciples— when they see the love you have for each other."

Your Focus on "Them" Will Make You the Cause of the Accident

December 2014 was full of reflections and lessons. One of the most memorable was the day that we had a surprise snowfall and ice blizzard. I had a meeting and by the time I left work, the weather had taken a turn for the worse. Within an hour, the roads were icy, and people were driving in a panic state. I remember looking in my rearview mirror while sitting at a red light, praying for God to slow down the car that was speeding up behind me. I was scared, and I had already envisioned the car running into me. The traffic light turned green before the car got close to me, and I immediately went from feeling scared to feeling angry, and now paranoid. I kept looking up at my mirror to keep an eye on how close this car was to me at every traffic light and stop sign. And despite my cautious driving, I slid and skidded on several patches of ice. There was a point when I had paid so much attention to the car behind me that I found myself driving closer to the car in front of me than I cared to be. At that moment, I took my focus off the car behind me and began to solely depend on God to guide my path home. I had to praise God for His grace and mercy.

Many of us have heard the analogy about driving forward while looking in the rearview mirror. This car incident sheds light on the fact that we can't make any progress in life, if we are focused on the wrong things. Sometimes, we just need to let go!

- I did not know the person driving that car. I had no connection to them at all. I prayed for God to keep me safe. When I saw the car speeding towards me, I asked God to slow them down. Instead of thanking God for answering my prayer, I became fixated on the person and not the blessing.
- No matter how badly I wanted to change how that driver was driving, I couldn't change it. I gave my attention and power away to a stranger that had no idea how upset I was.
- During all the craziness that was going on that day, God was still in control! I asked, and He provided. This is a part of building your faith. No need to keep focused on the problem if you have sincerely asked God to fix it. Worrying only negates your prayers.

Matthew 8:26 ESV "And he said to them, "Why are you afraid, O you of little faith?" Then he rose and rebuked the winds and the sea, and there was a great calm."

Good Fog

When the weatherman says "foggy and unclear skies" first thing in the morning, it can be really discouraging. I immediately panic because I know that means traffic will be heavy, and I may be late to work, school or wherever.

I am reminded of those times when I looked ahead at a situation and thought that something seemed like a really good idea or a once in a lifetime deal. I put the pedal to the medal and went full speed ahead. Unfortunately, that usually landed me in a ditch or mud puddle, and it took me some serious effort and strength to get out of it. God has a way of creating fog, forcing us to move with caution and care. The fog won't stop you, it will simply keep you focused on what's important at that moment. Stay focused on the future; however, don't do it at the expense of your current situation. Use discernment and pay attention to that gut feeling as you travel through life allowing God to be in control of your path and speed.

Philippians 3:15-21 (MSG) "So let's keep focused on that goal, those of us who want everything God has for us. If any of you have something else in mind, something less than total commitment, God will clear your blurred vision—you'll see it yet! Now that we're on the right track, let's stay on it."

Quick Question

Who are you PRAYING for?
What do you really BELIEVE?
How does your LIFE BLESS others?
When did you discover by FAITH you could achieve?
Why all these questions you ask?
WHY NOT?

My goal is to remind you to think about THE ONE who provides for you!

I pray that you will believe that you can make a difference. You can be the one thing that helps someone choose life. Your words can bless a person without them acknowledging it at that moment because they need time to process it. Remember that seeds do not grow the same day they are planted. Have faith that God is working behind the scenes to grant your request. I hope you will choose to encourage someone else to remember the same thing.

2 Chronicles 7:14 (NIV) "If my people, who are called by my name, will humble themselves and pray and seek my face and turn from their wicked ways, then I will hear from heaven, and I will forgive their sin and will heal their land."

The Life Cycle: Butterfly vs Human in Christ

Everybody wants to talk about the caterpillar and the butterfly, but nobody wants to tell what happens in the middle, before, or during that transformation. The entire life cycle is needed in order to have that magnificent ending. If you skip steps or attempt to cut them short, you risk having a deformed or underdeveloped life. Make the choice to stand firm and endure the entire process or be satisfied with getting remnants of the great life that God planned for you.

If you think back to your years in elementary school, you may remember exploring the butterfly's life cycle in detail. It may have been a simplified version depending on who was teaching it, but it included all four stages of its life. All butterflies must complete four stages to become an adult. Each stage has a different goal. Depending on the type of butterfly, the life cycle may take anywhere from one month to a whole year. I believe that disciples of Christ can share a similar transformation process.

The First Stage

- Butterfly: Lays her eggs on a leaf.
- Human: Introduced to Christ, accepts Him as Lord and Savior. Attends church with purpose. Starts to memorize key scriptures.

The Second Stage

- Butterfly: The egg hatches and the caterpillar will eat the leaf to grow and expand quickly from its' extremely small size.

- Human: Reads different versions of the bible for understanding. They attend Bible study and prays more often.

The Third Stage

- Butterfly: The Pupa (Chrysalis) caterpillar begins to transition. As soon as a caterpillar is fully grown, it transforms into a pupa, also known as a chrysalis. From the outside, it looks as if the caterpillar is resting, but there is a lot of action taking place on the inside. The caterpillar is rapidly changing. Within the chrysalis, the old body parts of the caterpillar are undergoing a remarkable transformation called metamorphosis. The caterpillar has completely transformed and now begins the final stage of the butterfly's life cycle.
- Human: They learn how to effectively communicate with God and seeks to understand their purpose for Kingdom work. They begin to truly understand the importance of witnessing and discipleship.

The Fourth Stage

- Butterfly: The adult butterfly emerges and is constantly on the lookout to reproduce, and the butterfly life cycle will continue when a female butterfly lays her eggs.
- Human: They absorb the task given by God and seeks ways to be a blessing to others. They have a clear understanding of the influence, and impact that their actions have on others. They share their story to encourage and inspire others to live for Christ.

The amazing life cycle of the butterfly is a great lesson for everyone to learn. It is not only a lesson that involves an ever-changing insect, but it is one about the transformation that can be applied to human lives as well. This transformation process gives us the visual needed to understand how a Christian can evolve and become a beautiful new creature. You can only fly if you follow the steps of our Creator. Be transparent and explain to others that not only do insects like the butterfly change and have stages of growth, but people change on the inside every day too.

2 Corinthians 5:17 (NIV) "Therefore, if anyone is in Christ, the new creation has come:[a] The old has gone, the new is here!"
2 Peter 1:5-11 (NIV) "For this very reason, make every effort to add to your faith goodness; and to goodness, knowledge; and to knowledge, self-control; and to self-control, perseverance; and to perseverance, godliness; and to godliness, mutual affection; and to mutual affection, love. For if you possess these qualities in increasing measure, they will keep you from being ineffective and unproductive in your knowledge of our Lord Jesus Christ. But whoever does not have them is nearsighted and blind, forgetting that they have been cleansed from their past sins. Therefore, my brothers and sisters, make every effort to confirm your calling and election. For if you do these things, you will never stumble, and you will receive a rich welcome into the eternal kingdom of our Lord and Savior Jesus Christ."

My Life...His way!

Please be patient, because God is not through with me yet.
I know I make lots of mistakes; however, it's all part of the plan that He has set.
You may not understand it, and that's okay too.
When He decided to make me, He wasn't considering you.
So please be patient with me, because my life is under construction.
God's building and creating a masterpiece, and only He has the instructions.

Isaiah 30:18 (TLB) "Yet the Lord still waits for you to come to Him, so he can show you his love; he will conquer you to bless you, just as he said. For the Lord is faithful to his promises. Blessed are all those who wait for him to help them."

New Me Coming Soon

I thought I had made it!

I just knew I had it all under control.

Then the weight of life's obstacles hit me, and my life started to unfold.

The ups and downs seemed unfair, and when it was happening I didn't know what to say.

A voice spoke ever so clearly saying, "Let's try it My way."

My weeping endured more than a night and finally, my days begin to seem clear.

That voice was God's reminder to always keep Him near.

I want what He wants for me, so I must follow His instructions.

Stay tuned for the new me coming soon, because my life is under construction.

Philippians 1:6 (NIV) "Be confident of this, that he who began a good work in you will carry it on to completion until the day of Christ Jesus."

Justice for All

You do not even know why I am crying.
You cannot even begin to understand my pain!
You said some words to try and comfort me,
But your words can not dissolve in my veins.
I cannot tell you how I feel.
I can only tell you I am growing numb!
I do not want to hear anything about how we shall overcome.
The words of many are dissolved by the actions of a few.
All I want is true justice for all because it is long overdue!
I wish I had an answer to make this all go away.
No! Real talk - I want those who caused this pain to get locked up and stay!
These wrongs make me want to write, so my words are fueled by something said by some.
I pray God will bless us all, but He will require us to get the work done!

Romans 12:19 (KJV) "Dearly beloved, avenge not yourselves, but rather give place unto wrath: for it is written, Vengeance is mine; I will repay, saith the Lord."

The Diary of a Grown-Up | Kathy Taylor

Dear Diary,

Reading through this chapter reminded me that....

God wants us to Love, Invest, build a Future, and Encourage others.

6

Career and B.O.S.S. Moves

Bold

Observant

Strategic

Successful

Dear Diary,

True leaders do not have to demand others to follow them. They present a plan that is so enticing that people follow just to find out more. When I am intentionally walking in my purpose, I have clarity that won't let others throw me off my course often. I can say with certainty, "I am who I say I am, and I am bold, observant, strategic, and successful in my moves."

-Kathy

If your success is defined by a purpose-driven mission, you will excel in spite of what your current situation looks like. Speak life and keep positive energy around you. After all, faith is the substance of things hoped for and the evidence of things unseen.

Hebrews 11:1 (NIV) "Now faith is confidence in what we hope for and assurance about what we do not see."

Amos 9:13-15 (MSG) "Yes indeed, it won't be long now." God's Decree. "Things are going to happen so fast your head will swim, one thing fast on the heels of the other. You won't be able to keep up. Everything will be happening at once and everywhere you look, blessings! Blessings like wine pouring off the mountains and hills. I'll make everything right again for my people Israel: "They'll rebuild their ruined cities. They'll plant vineyards and drink good wine. They'll work their gardens and eat fresh vegetables. And I'll plant them, plant them on their own land. They'll never again be uprooted from the land I've given them." God, your God, says so.

God-Style Confidence

I'm bold like that,
because He loves me like that.
I'm chilled like that,
because He gives me peace like that.
I believe like that,
because He provides for me like that.
I'm blessed like that,
because His favor is where it's at!

Proverbs 8:35-36 (MSG) "So, my dear friends, listen carefully; those who embrace my ways are most blessed. Mark a life of discipline and live wisely; don't squander your precious life. Blessed the man, blessed the woman, who listens to me, awake and ready for me each morning, alert and responsive as I start my day's work. When you find me, you find life, real life, to say nothing of God's good pleasure. But if you wrong me, you damage your very soul; when you reject me, you're flirting with death."

She Is Something Extra

Extraordinary, remarkable, and stunning is what they see.
She looks in the mirror, and humbly says, “It’s just me.”
She does not put on airs or pretend to talk about what she does not know.
Yet, the radiance she exudes has such a remarkable glow.
They rave about her exceptional style, and her amazing play on words.
She thinks it is just average and cannot hear exactly what they heard.
She has an unbelievable effect on others when she enters the room;
Her confidence and humble spirit alludes that she is very well groomed.
She begs for people not to sing her praises or honor her as if she has done some miraculous thing.
She remembers the day that she surrendered all, and accepted Jesus as her Savior and King.
From rags to riches was the transformation that happened within!
What others see is the product of a woman who freely repented from sin.
This woman doesn't hesitate to acknowledge that there's more to her than what they see.
This Phenomenal Woman proudly professes it is the GOD IN ME!

Psalm 139:14 (ESV) “I praise you, for I am fearfully and wonderfully made. Wonderful are your works; my soul knows it very well.”

Oh, They are Coming for You

Some time ago, I was asked, "How much capital would it take to fund your vision?" My first instinct was to throw out a number bigger than I had available; however, it made me think about the fact that I had never really done the math. That lead me to think more. Why haven't I ever done the math? My mind also wandered off to thoughts of shady behavior and backstabbing that often happens in "big business", and I didn't want to deal with that. But, guess what? Shady behavior and backstabbing happen in everyday small businesses too.

Let's acknowledge that "they" are coming, so we are no longer concerned about the assumption of "if," but we need to focus on the "when."

How does one prepare for the next level?

Get organized now. This way, when the unexpected comes, you won't be caught off guard. Be prepared to answer the detailed questions about your plans for the vision.

When they come, will you know what category to put them in?

There are friends, business partners, and acquaintances. For example, you cannot trust an acquaintance with your "deep dark secret past". It's not about trying to hide anything. They just don't have the connection or understanding needed to cover or protect you.

Putting an acquaintance in that position would be unfair to both persons involved.

The concern is not who is coming but what they are bringing.

Don't be naive and closed minded to think you know what all bad, jealous, haters, or imps look like. Stay focused on your goal and in tune with God so you will be able to make wise decisions regardless of what is coming your way. The person who can fund your vision may look like a homeless person or cast away. With the stroke of one check, your wildest dream could be paid in full!

Out of comfort and familiarity, we will bring inexperienced people to the business table. It is usually because of insecurities or doubts about who they are that makes them incapable of handling what is about to happen for you. Surround yourself with people who have a vision and are taking action towards fulfilling it.

Fear can rule your decisions on different levels.

Fear of the unknown: For example, if you can't see how "K" will connect to "A", you are likely to question if it's in the correct order. Later, you realize that even though "A" is several letters before "K" in the alphabet, you need "K" to come first to properly spell out the name, Kathy. What originally seemed odd or troubling at first, now makes complete sense.

Fear of Success: With success comes responsibility and some people will sabotage their own good fortune, thinking they know how to handle it without seeking wise counsel.

Fear of Failure: If I never try, then I won't fail. Not so! The truth is, you have already failed when you decide not to try.

There is no doubt that they are coming for you, however, when you are prepared and connected to God, you will be successful at living out your purpose.

Hebrews 12:2-3 (MSG) "Do you see what this means—all these pioneers who blazed the way, all these veterans cheering us on? It means we'd better get on with it. Strip down, start running—and never quit! No extra spiritual fat, no parasitic sins. Keep your eyes on Jesus, who both began and finished this race we're in. Study how he did it. Because he never lost sight of where he was headed—that exhilarating finish in and with God—he could put up with anything along the way: Cross, shame, whatever. And now he's there, in the place of honor, right alongside God. When you find yourselves flagging in your faith, go over that story again, item by item, that long litany of hostility he plowed through. That will shoot adrenaline into your souls!"

The Season of the Snowflake

It was another crazy day in December 2015 when it started snowing midday. It caused extremely dangerous traffic events throughout the city and chaos for local schools. I was in the middle of a major project at work and I had to find a good stopping point before I was comfortable heading to my nice warm home.

As I was driving home watching the snowflakes fall from the sky the traffic got worse. Many accidents had already happened. And as tempted as I was to complain about the traffic and crazy drivers, I decided in this moment to give thanks to God for granting me life to even see the snow. As I praised God, a shift happened, and my attitude became cheerful. This shift made it easier for me to hear God speak and give me insight.

As clear as I saw the big white flakes falling from the sky, I heard God's voice giving me an analogy: In every season it can be warm, rainy, or just a little chilly. It is only during the season of winter that snow is acceptable. Snow has a specific season and carries a unique look. Every other type of weather may not be desired; however, it is accepted.

God told me that there is a specific season for significant increase. It cannot happen off season, nor will it look like anything else. I must be prepared for the specific season of my greater, or I may have to wait for it to come back again. Keep in mind that there are three other seasons that must also take place before this one returns. I no longer want God to bring sunshine during my "snow season" just so that I can be comfortable. I want him to send the unique snowflakes that he created to be used in my favor!

Isaiah 55:8 (NLT) "My thoughts are nothing like your thoughts," says the LORD. "And my ways are far beyond anything you could imagine."

Are You Really Prepared

We often say, "If I had this, I would do that" or "If I had that, I would do this". Well, the truth is, if you do not work with what you have right now, you will never gain "this" or "that". Preparation and gratitude for the here and now is a great start for what is to come. You and I cannot keep asking for increased territory if we are not appreciative of what we currently have. I'm sure you can recall many times when you wished and prayed hard for something, and once you got it, you thought:

That's not what I really wanted after all. Then you start the quest all over again. Philippians 4:6 says, "Be anxious for nothing but in everything submit your request to God..." Our imagination often runs wild with expectations of others, and with ideas of how we think things should happen. Unfortunately, we don't know what's best for ourselves, and as long as we depend on our own understanding, we will continue to be off base and unprepared.

Remember, only God can send or provide the water. He just wants us to dig the ditches in order for it to have somewhere to go. Do the work now and be prepared for your blessing to overflow.

2 Corinthians 9:8 (NIV) "And God is able to bless you abundantly, so that in all things at all times, having all that you need, you will abound in every good work."

Malachi 3:10 (NIV) "Bring the whole tithe into the storehouse, that there may be food in my house. Test me in this," says the Lord Almighty, "and see if I will not throw open the floodgates of heaven and pour out so much blessing that there will not be room enough to store it."

Flip the Script

When they say, you can't do something and add malice to your name;
Don't feel obligated to straighten them, it's just a part of the game.
When the burden of everyone else's words starts to weigh heavy on you, remember what God's word says, and that's the only word destined to come true.
They may smile in your face and instigate attacks at your back;
Your silent prayers will prevail when God's word responds with the facts.
There is a calling on your life, and a purpose that you must achieve;
God said He has already supplied every tool that you will need.
Their negative words, and false statements may influence some;
Your life was predefined for greatness and your victory is already won!
So, when you're faced with a trial or obstacle, please remember this important tip;
Let God's word stand true, and He will flip the script.

Isaiah 54:17 (NKJV) "No weapon formed against you shall prosper, and every tongue which rises against you in judgment. You shall condemn. This is the heritage of the servants of the Lord, and their righteousness is from Me," says the Lord.

Your Uniqueness

Celebrate Your Uniqueness! Don't be envious of the runner in the lane next to you. Focus on finishing your own race. God wants you to enjoy using the gifts and talents He has given specifically to you. Satan will try to steal your joy from you by tempting you to compare yourself with others, and by trying to get you to conform to how others think you should do something, versus how God told you to do it. Be cautious and cognizant of your own thoughts and words, and the words of those around you. Do a self-check with God as often as needed to ensure you are on the right path.

Psalm 139:14 (NIV) "I praise you because I am fearfully and wonderfully made; your works are wonderful, I know that full well."

Dear Diary,

Reading through this chapter reminded me that I am...

"Bold, Observant, Strategic, and Successful"

7

Love, God

Dear Diary,

God is always ready to talk and listen to me; however, constant distractions, and life circumstances keep me from connecting with Him the way I should. This doesn't mean that I don't pray, serve, believe, or trust Him. It simply means that He could give me more direction if I had more uninterrupted conversations with Him. His wisdom surpasses my understanding, and I sometimes rush the processes of life to get to the familiar parts, so that I can remain comfortable.

-Kathy

God has a way of connecting with us on an individual level. He knows how to get our attention according to how He created us. He is willing to use a humorous phrase, a creative passage, or something else to get our attention. He promised to go to the end of the earth for us all because He loves us.

Trust me, I know what I am doing.
Love, God

Proverbs 3:5-6 (AMP) "Trust in and rely confidently on the Lord with all your heart and do not rely on your own insight or understanding. In all your ways know and acknowledge and recognize Him, And He will make your paths straight and smooth [removing obstacles that block your way]."

99 Problems

They said stuff!
You felt like you were not enough!
The job you wanted fell through!
Now you do not know what to do!
Bill collectors keep calling your phone!
It seems like the enemy will not leave you alone!
You are now questioning your faith!
You're not sure if you want to see another day!
You asked, "Why God? I can't take it no more!"
He replied, "I'm here. Search your core!
I will never leave nor forsake you my child!
I have been there all the while.
Just ask and you shall receive.
Renew your faith and believe.
I will not let your problems destroy you.
My grace and mercy will see you through.
Your reality counts problems and pain.
I count it all joy and the lessons gained!
You might see 99 problems but my love for you isn't one!"

Love, God

The Silent Healer

Remembering the goodness of God in the midst of adversity is not always an easy task. Many will say that you need to pray, and others will say they are praying for you. Overall, your mind is turning and trying to get past the "why me" moment. Scriptures come to mind, but suddenly you can't comprehend the meaning of the words. Where do you start? What do you do? How can you think past that moment? When does the healing process start? So many questions and not one answer seems to help. No one can console the hurt, pain, or confusion you have right now. And that's okay, because sometimes the answer is in the silence. Even though you know what pains you, you can't really figure out what to pray for. God is the only one that can heal you from the inside out. There's no need to talk about or explain the situation to others. Let God take the lead so that the healing can begin. Choose to trust God's word even when His word doesn't seem like enough.

Lamentations 3:22-30 (MSG) "God's loyal love couldn't have run out; His merciful love couldn't have dried up. They're created new every morning. How great your faithfulness! I'm sticking with God (I say it over and over. He's all I've got left. God proves to be good to the man who passionately waits, to the woman who diligently seeks. It's a good thing to quietly hope, quietly hope for help from God. It's a good thing when you're young to stick it out through the hard times. When life is heavy and hard to take, go off by yourself. Enter the silence. Bow in prayer. Don't ask questions: Wait for hope to appear.

Don’t run from trouble. Take it full-face. The “worst” is never the worst."

Easy Love

He makes love seem so easy.
He forgives and forgets with such grace.
He even sacrificed his son to save the human race.
He decided not to punish me the way I deserved.
He spoils me as if I am the one that should be served!
He rewards me with favor as if I have been extra good.
He soothes and holds me when I am down like no other could.
He is Him!
I call Him my King!
My King is the reason that I can proudly rejoice and sing!
He has risen.
He is alive and well.
He is the reason there is a story to tell.

John 3:16-18 (MSG) "This is how much God loved the world: He gave his Son, his one and only Son. And this is why: so that no one need be destroyed; by believing in him, anyone can have a whole and lasting life. God didn't go through all the trouble of sending his Son merely to point a finger, telling the world how bad it was. He came to help, to put the world right again. Anyone who trusts in him is acquitted; anyone who refuses to trust him has long since been under the death sentence without knowing it. And why? Because of that person's failure to believe in the one-of-a-kind Son of God when introduced to him."

He and I

He makes me smile for no specific reason.

He loves me throughout all my life seasons.

He protects me because I am his own.

He knows just what to say, and with a comforting tone.

To the one who truly loves me, I just want to say...

Thank you, Lord, for your favor and grace.

2 Corinthians 4:18 (NIV) "So we fix our eyes not on what is seen, but what is unseen. For what is seen is temporary, but what is unseen is eternal."

The Awkwardness of Being Alone

Everyone had someone to talk to except you. People were greeting each other and catching up. You accidentally met eyes with someone from across the room, and they gave the "Hey, how are you?" smile and nod. They stared a little while longer because they were not sure if they knew you. You returned the pleasantries and then looked down at your phone. Your feelings about leaving heightened because as you looked at your phone you noticed you only had one bar left. All of your goals had been accomplished for the night. You took a selfie, you checked in via Facebook and Instagram, and you purchased a t-shirt in support of the event. And yet, you still stayed seated. You were waiting for something, but you did not know what. You sat there awkwardly waiting and waiting. Constantly trying to distract yourself. You got so caught up in not trying to be noticed as an outsider that you didn't realize that everyone was leaving. During your waiting, you started writing to keep busy. At that moment, you noticed you wrote 'sitting still'. It didn't make sense immediately, but the message later became crystal clear.

A Message from God: In these moments when you feel alone I do my best work. You have to risk being awkward or the odd one because I need you set apart from the crowd. Do not get discouraged or frustrated by the difficulties that come with obeying my commands. No one can direct your path and guarantee your success like me. Sit still and know that I am God!

Psalm 46:10 (NIV) "He says, "Be still, and know that I am God; I will be exalted among the nations, I will be exalted in the earth."

Listen to Me

But I told you that it was going to be alright.
Love, God

When we try to fix our lives ourselves, we make a bigger mess of things. Having faith and believing that God has already mapped out your entire life journey means we don't have to figure it out alone. Let these scriptures serve as reminders that He already has a plan. You don't have to be anxious or concerned about the outcome when you do things His way.

Isaiah 55:8-9 (TLB) "This plan of mine is not what you would work out, neither are my thoughts the same as yours! For just as the heavens are higher than the earth, so are my ways higher than yours, and my thoughts than yours."

Philippians 4:6 (GNT) "Don't worry about anything, but in all your prayers ask God for what you need, always asking him with a thankful heart."

Numbers 14:11-12 (GNT) The LORD said to Moses, "How much longer will these people reject me? How much longer will they refuse to trust in me, even though I have performed so many miracles among them? I will send an epidemic and destroy them, but I will make you the father of a nation that is larger and more powerful than they are!"

Psalm 12:6 (GNT) "The promises of the Lord can be trusted; they are as genuine as silver refined seven times in the furnace."

I Got This

It may seem like everyone is against you but, that's not true. I am just protecting your future and my investment.

Love, God

Haters, naysayers, opposers, and negative people seem to overpower our judgment and actions at times. It is easy to get discouraged and question why this happens. Especially, when it seems like nothing is working, and no one is supporting you. This is the perfect time to press into God and His word. Remember that weapons and opposition are inevitable; however, they will not win if you stay focused on God and His plan. I hope these scriptures remind you that no one, or thing can take away His promise, purpose, or plan, for your life.

1 Corinthians 10:13 (MSG) "No test or temptation that comes your way is beyond the course of what others have had to face. All you need to remember is that God will never let you down; he'll never let you be pushed past your limit; he'll always be there to help you come through it."

Deuteronomy 31:6 (GNT) "Be determined and confident. Do not be afraid of them. Your God, the Lord himself, will be with you. He will not fail you or abandon you."

Psalm 34:17-20 (NIV) "The righteous cry out, and the Lord hears them; he delivers them from all their troubles. The Lord is close to the brokenhearted and saves those who are crushed in spirit. The righteous person may have many troubles, but the Lord delivers him from them all; he protects all his bones, not one of them will be broken."

Believe

Do you really believe me?

Love, God

If someone asked a group of Christians if they believe God can do anything, most would likely say "Yes" without hesitation. But, how do our words and actions match that of an unconditional faith, one that believes He really can do anything? Unconditional faith is believing without doubt or fear. Your faith should not be based on achieving the results that you desire, but simply trusting that God is always working on your behalf. Most of us put conditions on our faith in order to keep even a minimal portion of the control.

When writing this book, I had to face my fear of being open to others reading my personal words on a larger scale. I tried to modify what God told me to do by just writing and posting on a blog. That was not successful because that's not what He told me to do. When you do what the Word of God says, He's going to be faithful to His promises. There is nothing He cannot do, and you can do all things through Him!

The shift of your belief system has to happen in your mind before it can manifest on earth. If you cannot even write down the details of what you want to do, how do you begin to believe and have faith that it will become a reality? We've all downsized dreams and goals because it seemed too far out of reach. The stretch it would take to achieve such lofty accomplishments seems like a setup for possible ridicule, judgment, and failure. Instead of pushing towards the full fledge vision, we choose to create a modified version of it. This watered-down version is still a stretch, and it seems more realistic in comparison. Complete obedience to God often may seem like an unrealistic option, but it is so worth it.

When you really believe that God rules over heaven and earth, you will not downsize your dreams, goals, and visions. He can make anything happen. This book is proof of that!

Genesis 18:14 (NIV) "Is anything too hard for the Lord? I will return to you at the appointed time next year, and Sarah will have a son."
Jeremiah 32:17 (GNT) "Sovereign Lord, you made the earth and the sky by your great power and might; nothing is too difficult for you."

Dear Diary,

Reading through this chapter has shown me....

Scriptures and Resources

You Matter To God

It is my hope that many conversations will be prompted from reading this book. The most important conversation is the one you should have with God. If you have never accepted God into your life, please consider doing that now. Acts 2:21 says "Whosoever shall call on the name of the Lord shall be saved". Now is a good time to repent of your sin, ask God for forgiveness, and state belief in the life, death, and saving resurrection of Jesus Christ. Romans 10:9-10 says that "if you declare with your mouth, "Jesus is Lord," and believe in your heart that God raised him from the dead, you will be saved. For it is with your heart that you believe and are justified, and it is with your mouth that you profess your faith and are saved." Yes, it's that simple! God is a forgiving God, and He will forgive and accept you immediately. If you do this, the Bible says that your eternal salvation is secure!

Your next step would be to find a trusted source to talk to. I encourage you to find a local church where you can be baptized and grow in the knowledge of God through His Word, the Bible.

Romans 5:8 "But God showed his great love for us by sending Christ to die for us while we were still sinners."
Romans 10:9-10 (NIV) "If you declare with your mouth, "Jesus is Lord," and believe in your heart that God raised him from the dead, you will be saved. 10 For it is with your heart that you believe and are justified, and it is with your mouth that you profess your faith and are saved."

1 Corinthians 15:3-4 (NLT) "I passed on to you what was most important and what had also been passed on to me. Christ died for our sins, just as the Scriptures said. He was buried, and he was raised from the dead on the third day, just as the Scriptures said."

Scriptures

The Bible is filled with promises from our Creator. God is faithful and will fulfill all His promises. Make the choice to read and trust His word. Here are a few scriptures that stand out to me about his promises, encouragement, and forgiveness.

Scriptures of Promises

Isaiah 41:10 "So do not fear, for I am with you; do not be dismayed, for I am your God. I will strengthen you and help you; I will uphold you with my righteous right hand."
2 Chronicles 7:14 "if my people, who are called by my name, will humble themselves and pray and seek my face and turn from their wicked ways, then I will hear from heaven, and I will forgive their sin and will heal their land."
Philippians 4:19 "And my God will meet all your needs according to the riches of his glory in Christ Jesus."
Matthew 6:31-33 "So do not worry, saying, 'What shall we eat?' or 'What shall we drink?' or 'What shall we wear?' For the pagans run after all these things, and your heavenly Father knows that you need them. But seek first his kingdom and his righteousness, and all these things will be given to you as well."
Luke 11:9-13 "So I say to you: Ask and it will be given to you; seek and you will find; knock and the door will be opened to you. For everyone who asks receives; the one who seeks finds; and to the one who knocks, the door will be opened. "Which of you fathers, if your son

asks fora fish, will give him a snake instead? Or if he asks for an egg, will give him a scorpion? If you then, though you are evil, know how to give good gifts to your children, how much more will your Father in heaven give the Holy Spirit to those who ask him!"

Scriptures of Encouragement

1 Thessalonians 5:11 "Therefore encourage one another and build each other up, just as in fact you are doing."

Isaiah 40:31 "but those who hope in the LORD will renew their strength. They will soar on wings like eagles; they will run and not grow weary, they will walk and not be faint."

Joshua 1:9 "Have I not commanded you? Be strong and courageous. Do not be afraid; do not be discouraged, for the LORD your God will be with you wherever you go."

Proverbs 18:10 "The name of the LORD is a fortified tower; the righteous run to it and are safe."

Psalm 31:24 "Be strong and take heart, all you who hope in the LORD."

2 Corinthians 1:3-4 "Praise be to the God and Father of our Lord Jesus Christ, the Father of compassion and the God of all comfort, who comforts us in all our troubles, so that we can comfort those in any trouble with the comfort we ourselves receive from God."

Isaiah 41:10 "So do not fear, for I am with you; do not be dismayed, for I am your God. I will strengthen you and help you; I will uphold you with my righteous right hand."

John 14:27 "Peace I leave with you; my peace I give you. I do not give to you as the world gives. Do not let your hearts be troubled and do not be afraid."

John 16:33 "I have told you these things, so that in me you may have peace. In this world you will have trouble. But take heart! I have overcome the world."

Psalm 46:1-3 "God is our refuge and strength, an ever-present help in trouble. Therefore, we will not fear, though the earth give way and the mountains fall into the heart of the sea, though its waters roar and foam and the mountains quake with their surging."

Scriptures on Forgiveness

Colossians 3:13 "Bear with each other and forgive one another if any of you has a grievance against someone. Forgive as the Lord forgave you."

Matthew 6:14-15 "For if you forgive other people when they sin against you, your heavenly Father will also forgive you. But if you do not forgive others their sins, your Father will not forgive your sins."

Ephesians 4:31-32 "Get rid of all bitterness, rage and anger, brawling and slander, along with every form of malice. Be kind and compassionate to one another, forgiving each other, just as in Christ God forgave you."

1 John 1:9 "If we confess our sins, he is faithful and just and will forgive us our sins and purify us from all unrighteousness."

2 Corinthians 5:17 "Therefore, if anyone is in Christ, the new creation has come: The old has gone, the new is here!"

Ephesians 1:7 "In him we have redemption through his blood, the forgiveness of sins, in accordance with the riches of God's grace."

Daniel 9:9 "The Lord our God is merciful and forgiving, even though we have rebelled against him;"

Psalm 103:12 "as far as the east is from the west, so far has he removed our transgressions from us."

Mark 11:25 "And when you stand praying, if you hold anything against anyone, forgive them, so that your Father in heaven may forgive you your sins."

Resources

These are just a few of the websites I use to study God's word.

www.Biblestudytools.com
www.Biblegateway.com
www.Biblehub.com
www.Youversion.com (the app)
www.Navigators.org
www.Bible.org

Made in the USA
Coppell, TX
02 November 2021